GOLDIE IS A FISH

Millions of goldfish spend their lives in homes, schoolrooms, libraries, and public aquaria. To most children these fish are interesting pets, but grownups may see them as beautiful creatures that do not demand much care. Other grownups make them a hobby by rearing unusual varieties.

Still, goldfish are more than pets, ornaments, or a hobby. The little creatures are typical fish, which tell us much about other kinds that live in streams, ponds, lakes, and oceans. Watching Goldie or her relatives, we can discover what fish are, how they swim and breathe, and why some of them take long journeys though others seldom leave home. We find that some fish walk, climb, and even fly, though others spend long hours lying on mud or sand.

This account of Goldie and her fish-relatives is told in words familiar to third-graders. Rhythmic prose provides short lines, yet keeps the text from becoming a sequence of short, staccato sentences. Facts and principles can be understood by young readers, yet their meaning will increase as those readers grow older and learn more and more about the living world.

Dr. Fenton is widely known as an author, naturalist, and illustrator. Besides writing GOLDIE, he has provided the book with eighteen full-page illustrations and nine of smaller size.

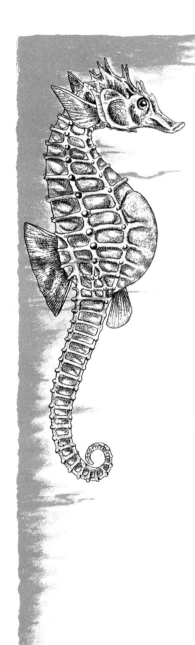

GOLDIE

IS A FISH

By Carroll Lane Fenton

Illustrated by the author

The John Day Company   New York

CONTENTS

Two other
goldfish

Goldie

Goldie and two other goldfish.

GOLDIE IS A FISH

Goldie is a goldfish.
She lives in a glass tank full of water
which we call an aquarium (a KWARE i um).
Other goldfish also live in the tank,
but they do not look like Goldie.
Some have long fins and tails,
or eyes that stick out from their heads.
Some are black, or silvery, or spotted
but never are orange or golden-yellow.
Let's look at Goldie and her neighbors.
Let's find out what they can tell
about fish that live in rivers and creeks —
about fish in ponds, lakes, and oceans,
as well as fish in aquariums.

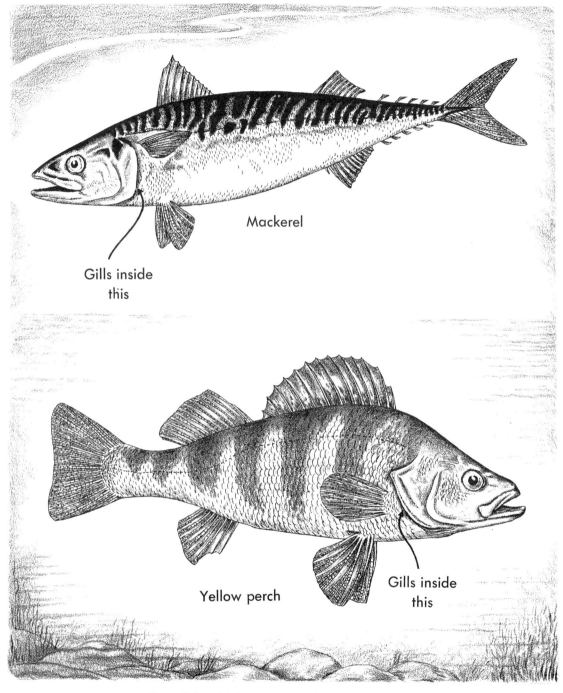

Mackerel

Gills inside
this

Yellow perch

Gills inside
this

Two fish which most people know.

WHAT ARE FISH?

Goldie is a goldfish.
She swims, and eats, and lives in the water.
Her backbone is made up of many pieces.
She wears scales, not hair, on her skin,
which is covered with slippery slime.
Goldie has fins instead of legs.
She breathes with things called gills,
which are in her body, back of her head
and are covered with wide, thin bones.
We say that Goldie is cold-blooded
because she never feels warm.
Fish are cold-blooded creatures
with gills, slippery skins, backbones,
and fins instead of legs.

SOME "FISH" ARE NOT FISH

If fish always have backbones
what are starfish, jellyfish, crayfish,
and the things we often call shellfish?
They are animals without backbones
that got their names long, long ago
when "fish" meant almost any creature
that lived in the water.
A jellyfish is not at all like Goldie.
Jellyfish are soft and watery
and they never have fins or gills.
Starfish have stiff, prickly bodies

Starfish

Two
Jellyfish

that divide into parts called "arms."
Crayfish (also called crawfish or crawdads)
look like little lobsters
with jointed bodies and legs.
Oysters and clams are called shellfish,
but their shells and soft bodies tell us
that they are related to snails.
No grown-up oyster ever goes swimming,
because it has no fins.

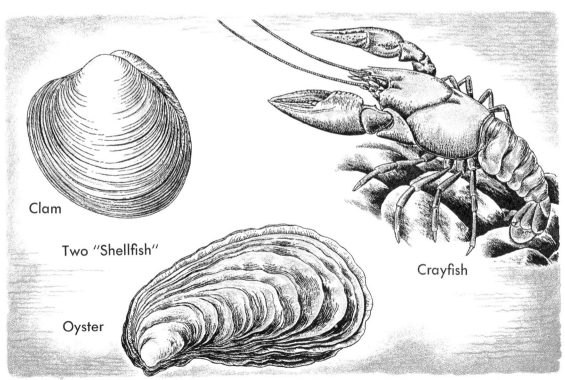

Clam

Two "Shellfish"

Oyster

Crayfish

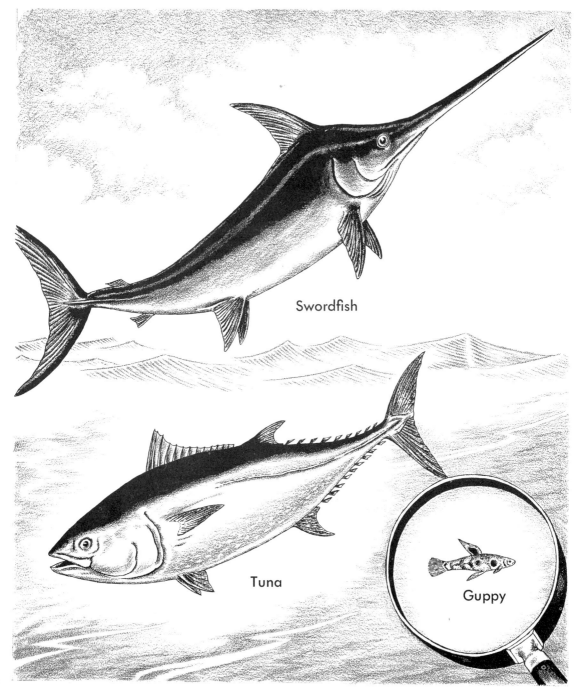

Swordfish

Tuna

Guppy

Big and little fish.

LITTLE AND BIG

Goldie is only three inches long.
Guppies are often less than one inch.
A few fish are smaller than guppies,
but many other kinds are larger.
Some big fish live in lakes or rivers,
but the largest kinds swim in the ocean.
Swordfish and tuna are two ocean fish
that become 10, 12, or 14 feet long
and weigh 1,000 pounds.
Some white sharks are 30 feet in length,
and whale sharks become still larger.
Whale sharks never harm people,
but white sharks are so fierce
that we often call them "man-eaters."

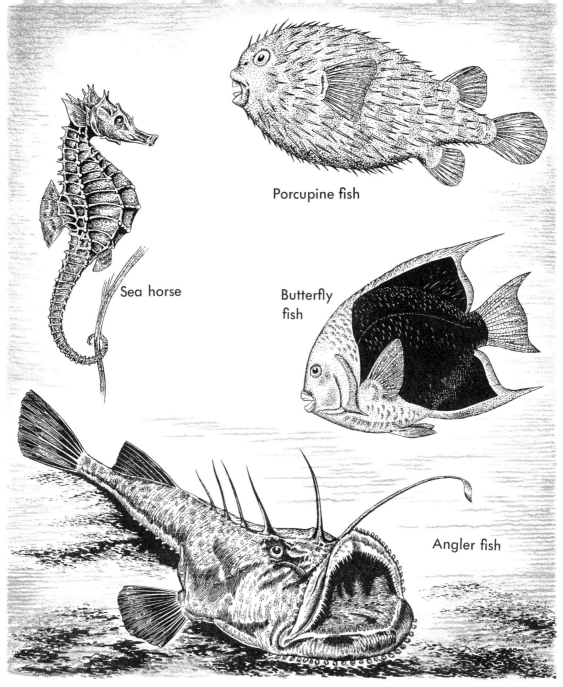

Porcupine fish

Sea horse

Butterfly
fish

Angler fish

These fish are not streamlined.

FISH HAVE DIFFERENT SHAPES

We often say that Goldie is streamlined.
This means that her body is shaped
so it goes through water easily.
Most other fish are streamlined, too,
but some kinds have different shapes.
Here are four of these different fish.
The porcupine fish is thick and short,
with sharp spines on his skin.
Butterfly fish are deep-bodied and thin.
The angler fish has a flattened body
that helps him lie on the sea bottom.
The sea horse does not look like a fish,
with his long spiny head, his rough body,
and his tail that curls around plants.

This golden trout is leaping to catch an insect.

Brook trout

Most fish swim with their bodies.

HOW FISH SWIM

You have legs and walk on land,
but Goldie swims in the water.
She swims by bending her body and tail
to one side and then to the other.
Most fish swim as Goldie does.
When they bend slowly, they swim slowly.
When they bend their bodies quickly
they swim faster and faster,
or even leap into the air.
When these fish want to stop
they spread their fins sideways.
Fish also spread their fins sideways
and move them slowly
when they want to stay in one place.

SWIMMING WITH FINS

Goldie swims by bending her body,
but the porcupine fish wiggles its tail,
and a sea horse moves the fin on its back.
Some fish that usually swim like Goldie
move slowly by rippling fins on their backs
or on their undersides.
The bowfin is one fish that does this,
but skates and rays have broad bodies
and their fins spread sideways.

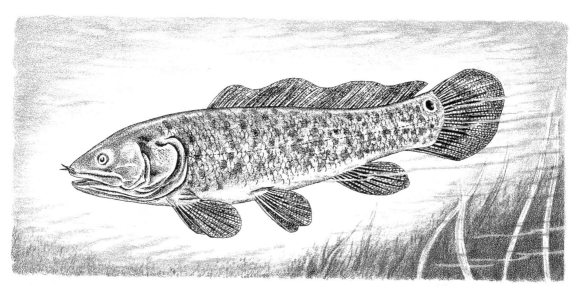

This bowfin is using the fin on its back.

These broad fish cannot bend
from one side to the other,
so they move their fins up and down.
The fish often look as if they were flying
when they use their fins to swim.

Skates and rays swim with fins at their sides.

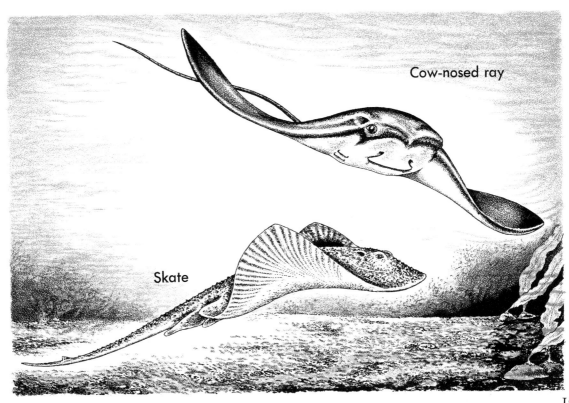

Cow-nosed ray

Skate

BONES AND NO BONES

Goldie has bones in her fins
and many, many bones in her body.
We call these bones her skeleton.
Goldie's skeleton (SKEL i tun)
keeps her body in shape,
even when she is out of the water.
If we could see through a bony fish
its skeleton would look
like the picture on this page.

The skeleton of a bony fish.

All sorts of fish have skeletons
but sharks and skates and rays are not bony.
A shark's skeleton is made
of tough white material
which we call cartilage (KAR ti lij).
Cartilage is not hard, like bone.
It keeps a shark's body in shape
while he is in the water.
But sharks feel soft
and lose their streamlined form
when they are caught
and are pulled out on land.

This shark has a skeleton,
but it is not made of bone.

Trunkfish

Gar, or gar pike

Armored catfish

Three fish with armor.

FISH WITH ARMOR

Knights of old often wore armor
made of steel pieces fastened together
with joints that let the men move.
Some fish wear armor, too,
but it is made of bone, not steel.
One armored fish is the gar.
Its skin is covered with bony scales
that are thick and very hard.
Armored catfish have plates of bone
that overlap and let the fish bend
when they swim.
The armor of trunkfish is solid,
except near the tail.
Trunkfish can wiggle their tails,
but they cannot bend their bodies
when they want to turn.

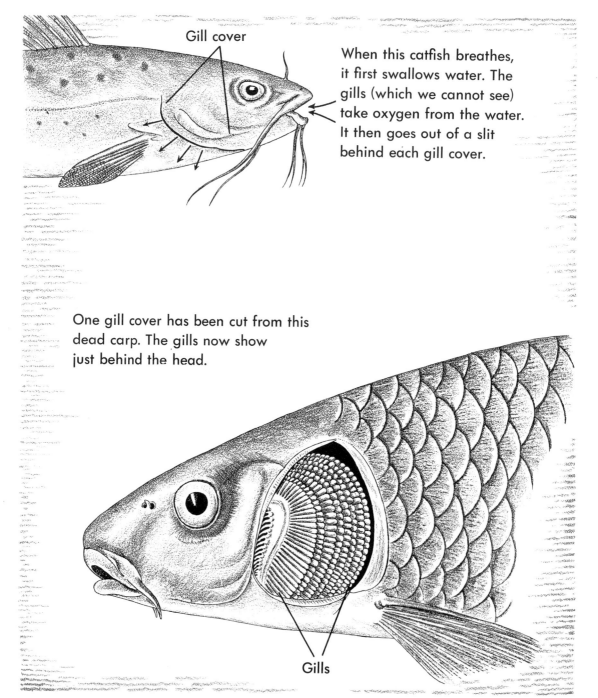

Gill cover

When this catfish breathes, it first swallows water. The gills (which we cannot see) take oxygen from the water. It then goes out of a slit behind each gill cover.

One gill cover has been cut from this dead carp. The gills now show just behind the head.

Gills

Gills and how they work.

BREATHING WITH GILLS

We breathe air into our lungs,
which take a gas called oxygen (OK si jen)
and let it go into our blood.
Goldie's blood needs oxygen, too,
but she gets it with gills
which breathe in the water.
You cannot see Goldie's gills
because they are covered by thin bones
at the back of her head.
But you can see the gills of fish
which Mother buys at the market
and prepares for cooking.
Ask her to cut off the gill covers.
Then use the picture on page 24
to find out how gills work.

Two lungfish swallowing air.

FISH THAT BREATHE AIR

The water in Goldie's bowl
is always kept fresh and clean.
But some wild fish live in water
that often becomes stale or dirty
and loses its oxygen.
The fish cannot breathe in stale water,
so they swim to the surface
and swallow air.
Bowfins and gars often do this,
and so do dark-colored lungfish.
Lungfish swallow air so well
that they never use their gills.
When ponds dry up, these fish live
in mud instead of water.

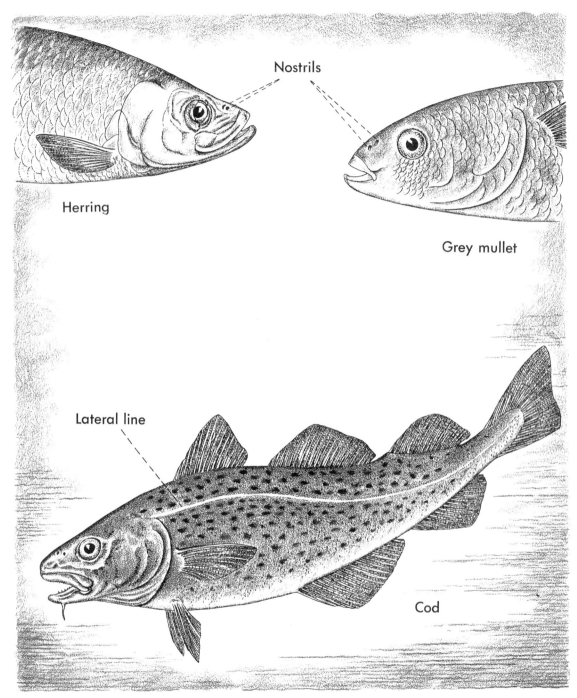

Nostrils

Herring

Grey mullet

Lateral line

Cod

Eyes, nostrils, and lateral line.

SEEING AND HEARING

Goldie sees with her big eyes.
She smells with two nostrils
near the front of her head.
Goldie can also taste things,
but her ears are inside her head
where they cannot hear well.
Fish also have little tubes
called lateral (LAT er ul) lines
along each side of the body.
Lateral lines feel low sounds
and tell whether the water
is growing warm or turning cool.
We can see Goldie's lateral lines,
but they show more plainly on cod,
and many other fish.

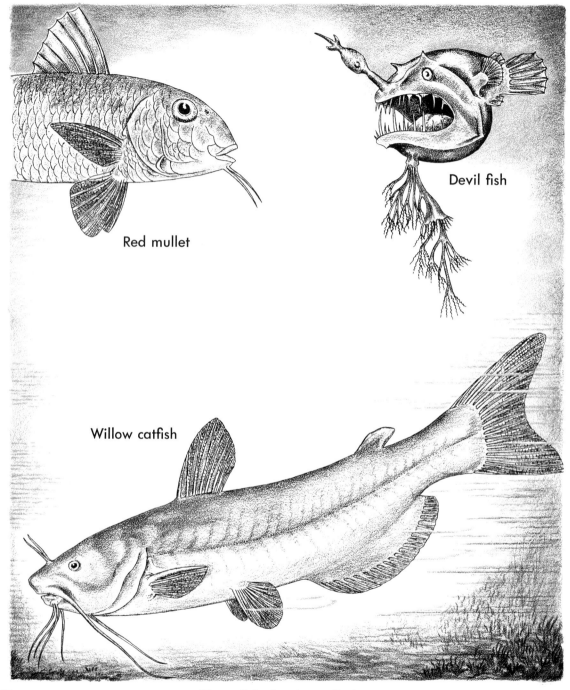

Red mullet

Devil fish

Willow catfish

Three fish that have feelers.

FEELERS

When we want to feel something
we touch it with our fingers.
Goldie cannot do this
because fish have fins, not hands.
Of course, some fish have feelers
on their fins or heads.
Codfish and drum have short feelers,
but those of the mullet are longer.
Catfish have long, thin feelers
that reach under stones or plants.
The longest feelers belong to fish
that live in deep, dark seas.
Some deep-sea fish have feelers
that hang down and branch like plants.
Other feelers look like whiplashes
that are longer than the fish.

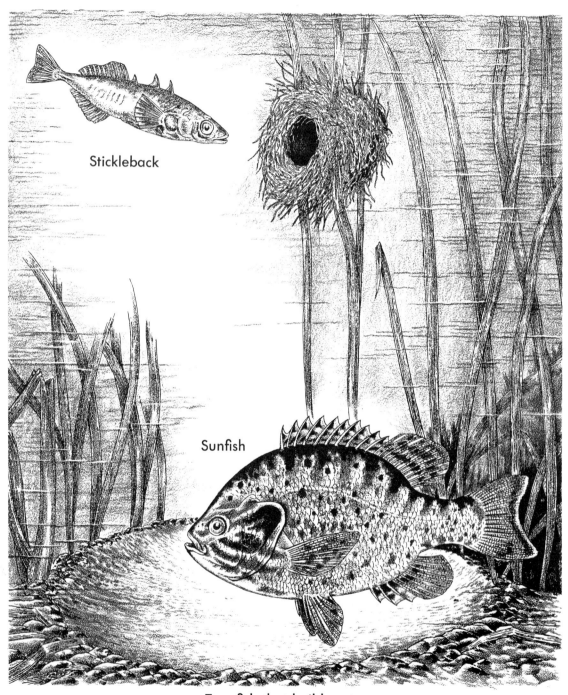

Stickleback

Sunfish

Two fish that build nests.

EGGS AND NESTS

Goldfish lay tiny, soft eggs
on plants that float in the water.
Other fish lay little eggs, too,
and put them in different places.
Codfish eggs float in the ocean,
but herring eggs are stuck
to small stones on the sea bottom.
Trout and salmon lay their eggs
in clear streams.
Bowfins, bullheads, and sunfish
dig saucer-shaped nests
in lakes, ponds, and slow rivers.
Mother fish lay their eggs in the nests.
Father fish take care of them
until the baby fish hatch.

Spotted dogfish and
three of its eggs.

Skate's eggs

A spotted dogfish and "sea purse" eggs.

MORE ABOUT EGGS

Goldfish eggs are little,
but a few fish lay large eggs.
Small sharks known as dogfish
lay large eggs with horny covers
which are often called sea purses.
Every "purse" has four twisty arms
that hold to seaweeds.
Some skates lay sea purses, too,
but they have stiff arms that stick
into sand on the sea bottom.
Other sharks, skates, and rays
have eggs that hatch
in the mother's body.
Then the baby fish come out
as if they were being born.

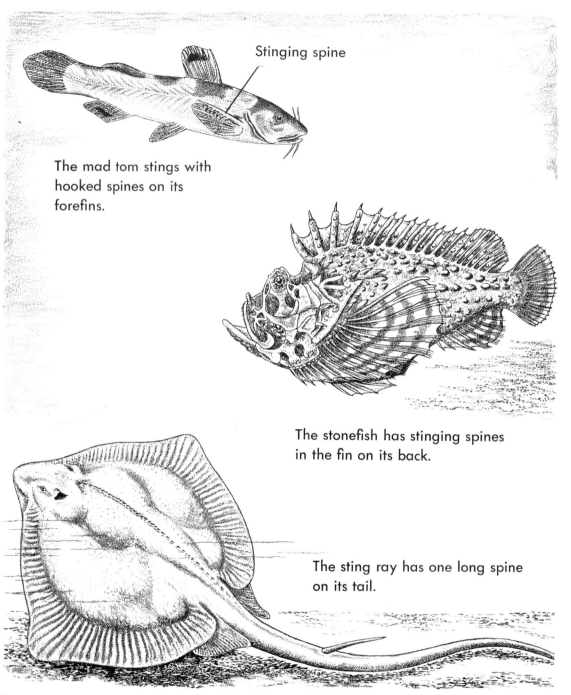

Stinging spine

The mad tom stings with
hooked spines on its
forefins.

The stonefish has stinging spines
in the fin on its back.

The sting ray has one long spine
on its tail.

Some fish that sting.

FISH THAT STING

Goldie is a harmless pet,
but some fish can bite fiercely
and others have spines that sting.
The mad tom stings with two spines—
one on each forefin.
Sharp, curved hooks on these spines
put poison, or venom, into creatures
that catch hold of mad toms.
The sting ray has one long spine
on his whip-shaped tail,
but spines of the ugly stonefish
are part of the fin on his back.
Poison on these spines is so strong
that it sometimes kills people
who go wading and step on stonefish.

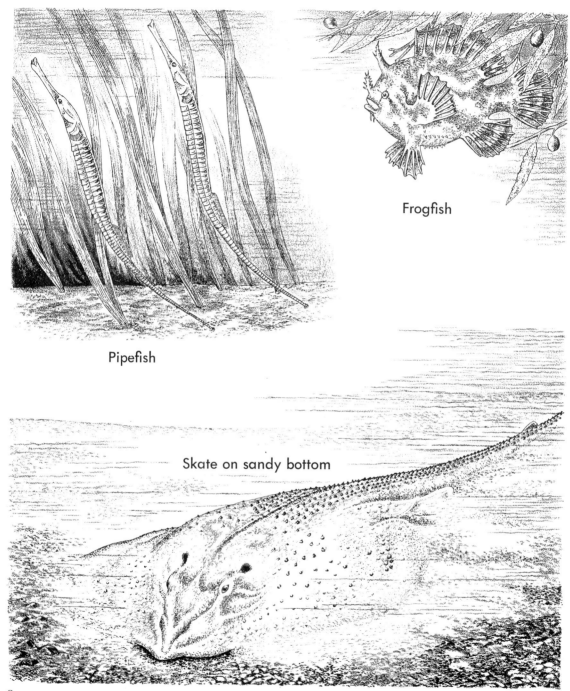

Frogfish

Pipefish

Skate on sandy bottom

38   Three ways of hiding.

HIDING

Eels catch their food at night.
When day comes, they crawl into sand
where other fish cannot see them.
Pipefish hide by swaying to and fro
so their slender green bodies
look like the plants around them.
Skates and rays hide easily, too,
because they are dull and flat.
A skate or ray flips its broad fins
when it settles down on the bottom.
Each flip stirs up sand
that falls upon the creature's skin.
Soon he looks like part of the bottom,
not like a living fish.

40 Three fish that live deep in the ocean.

DEEP-SEA FISH

Goldie likes her aquarium,
where the water is a few inches deep.
But many different wild fish live
far down in seas and oceans.
Some deep-sea fish are long and thin,
and look like silvery-white ribbons.
Other deep-sea fish are small,
and are dark brown, black, or purple.
Many small, dark fish
have round goggle eyes, wide mouths,
and long teeth that are
almost as sharp as needles.
Some kinds also have stomachs
that stretch and s-t-r-e-t-c-h
till they look like plastic bags
full of things the fish have eaten.

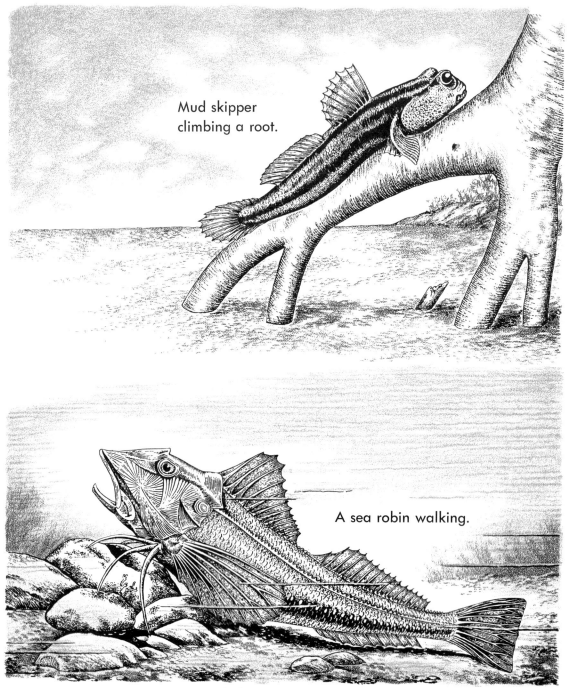

Mud skipper
climbing a root.

A sea robin walking.

Fish that walk and climb.

FISH THAT WALK

Goldie has fins and swims,
and so do sea robins.
But sea robins also walk.
They walk under water with bones
that look like long claws.
Mud skippers go walking, too,
but they do so on land.
Mud skippers live in pools
near hot, tropical seashores.
On sunny days the fish come out
to catch insects on land.
Mud skippers move swiftly
among weeds and over rocks.
Often the fish climb into low trees
that grow along the shore.

Flying fish

Flying gurnard

44   Two kinds of fish that fly.

SOME FISH FLY

Sea robins and mud skippers walk,
but some fish fly with fins
that spread out
like the wings of an airplane.
When one of these fish wants to fly
it swims faster and faster and FASTER
until it darts out of the water.
Then the fish spreads its wing-fins
and glides through the air.
Flying gurnards never glide very far
and they do not go very high.
Real flying fish glide much farther —
as far as one or two city blocks.
Flying fish sometimes go so high
that they fall on the decks
of ships.

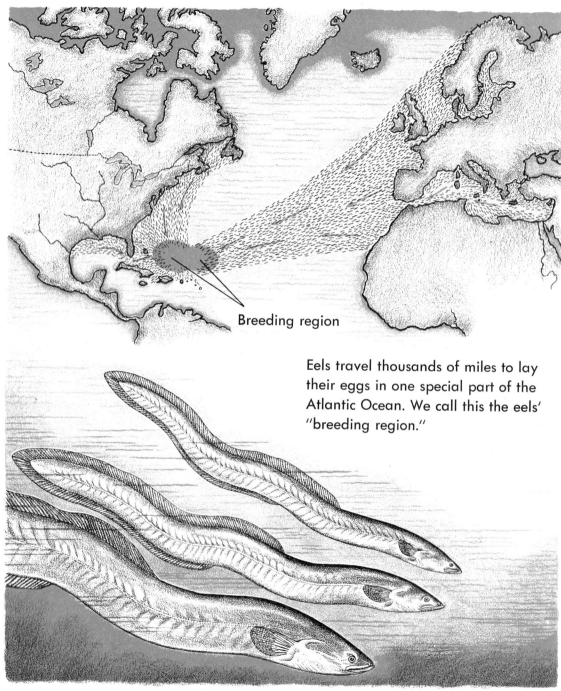

Breeding region

Eels travel thousands of miles to lay their eggs in one special part of the Atlantic Ocean. We call this the eels' "breeding region."

Eels are famous travelers.

FISH THAT TRAVEL

Goldie never leaves her aquarium,
but many kinds of wild fish
are famous travelers.
Some herring swim hundreds of miles
to find food or lay their eggs.
Mackerel live near shore in the summer
but go far out to sea in the fall.
Salmon hatch in lakes or streams.
Then they go to live in the ocean
but come back when they are grown.
Eels grow up in rivers
but go to the ocean to lay their eggs.
The map on page 46 shows how eels
come from North America and Europe
and travel to the part of the ocean
in which their eggs are laid.

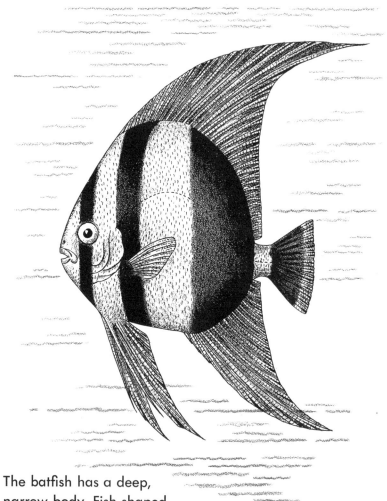

The batfish has a deep,
narrow body. Fish shaped
like this live among coral
reefs.

4632